THRILL SEEKERS

RACING THE IDITAROD

BY KRISTEN RAJCZAK

Gareth Stevens
Publishing

Please visit our website, www.garethstevens.com. For a free color catalog of all our high-quality books, call toll free 1-800-542-2595 or fax 1-877-542-2596.

Library of Congress Cataloging-in-Publication Data

Rajczak, Kristen.
Racing the Iditarod / by Kristen Rajczak.
   p. cm. — (Thrill seekers)
Includes index.
ISBN 978-1-4824-3291-6 (pbk.)
ISBN 978-1-4824-3292-3 (6-pack)
ISBN 978-1-4339-9902-4 (library binding)
1. Iditarod National Historic Trail (Alaska) — History — Juvenile literature. 2. Iditarod (Race) — Juvenile literature. 3. Sled dogs — Alaska — Juvenile literature. 4. Sled dog racing — Alaska — Juvenile literature. I. Rajczak, Kristen. II. Title.
SF440.15 R35 2014
798.8—dc23

First Edition

Published in 2014 by
Gareth Stevens Publishing
111 East 14th Street, Suite 349
New York, NY 10003

Copyright © 2014 Gareth Stevens Publishing

Designer: Michael J. Flynn
Editor: Therese Shea

Photo credits: Cover, pp. 1, 5–7, 15, 17, 19–21, 23, 25, 27, 29 Anchorage Daily News/McClatchy-Tribune/Getty Images; pp. 9, 11 AFP/Getty Images; p. 10 Matt Cooper/Shutterstock.com; p. 13 M. Gebicki/Lonely Planet Images/Getty Images; p. 24 Simon Bruty/Sports Illustrated/Getty Images.

Printed in the United States of America

CPSIA compliance information: Batch #CW14GS: For further information contact Gareth Stevens, New York, New York at 1-800-542-2595.

CONTENTS

Words in the glossary appear in **bold** type
the first time they are used in the text.

FEEL THE COLD

Imagine crossing through the frozen Alaska and Kuskokwim mountain ranges on the back of a dogsled. You stand on the **runners** as your team tries not to slip on the ice-covered Norton Sound. All around you, the **unpredictable** Alaskan winter warns of terrible weather. This is the Iditarod Trail Sled Dog Race.

Each March since 1973, the famous race's finish line has drawn hundreds of adventurous **mushers** to drive teams of 12 to 16 dogs over snow, slush, and mud. These bold men and women have braved whiteout snowstorms, pounding rain, and blinding sunlight.

The Great Race of Mercy

In 1925, a great blizzard struck in Alaska during an **epidemic**. Though dogsleds weren't used much by then, no airplanes could fly in the snow. A team of mushers carried medicine to Nome, Alaska, saving many lives. The modern Iditarod race is held partly to honor this historic event.

Lovers of dogsled racing call the Iditarod the "last great race on Earth."

Finishing the Iditarod is a challenging feat. Many who attempt the 1,100-mile (1,770 km) race between Anchorage and Nome, Alaska, fail. They, or their dogs, become ill from little sleep and lack of food. And spending more than a week—sometimes as many as 3 weeks—mostly alone in the wilderness takes a mental toll.

So, why race the Iditarod? Some people love the danger of the trail! Others honor the tradition of sled dogs bringing mail to gold mining camps in the early 1900s. But, of course, there's also the glory—and about $600,000 of prize money—waiting for the finishers!

In 2013, 54 mushers finished the race. Twelve others started but didn't finish.

Dependable Dogs

Joe Redington, one of the Iditarod founders, said, "I didn't like that I've seen snow machines break down and fellows freeze to death out there in the wilderness. But dogs will always keep you warm and they'll always get you there." Since his death in 1999, Redington's name has been called during Iditarod board meetings. "Joe is on the trail," the members say.

RACE RULES

In order to compete in the Iditarod today, mushers must be 18 years old. A musher must have finished an earlier Iditarod, the Yukon Quest International Sled Dog Race, or two 300-mile (483 km) qualifying races plus one other qualifying race to equal 750 miles (1,207 km). An Iditarod review board checks applicants' qualifications carefully—and they're allowed to turn down entries!

The rules state: "The race should be won or lost by the musher and dogs on merit rather than on **technicalities**." That means a team should win because of its abilities and not because of a minor rule. Therefore, training is very important!

Restart

The Iditarod starting line in Anchorage is surrounded by fun events and people having a good time. All the teams run a short first part of the race, but it's just to get to the "restart" line. The timed race starts the following day. Teams begin the race with a few minutes between them.

The Iditarod rules say a bit about how mushers should and shouldn't compete in the race. For example, the Good Samaritan rule says a musher may help another team in an **emergency**.

TEAM IN TRAINING

Iditarod sled dogs may start training as puppies. Early on, they learn to trust and look to their musher for leadership. At around 6 months old, the puppies can wear a **harness** for the first time. Then, the dogs begin learning about pulling a sled and racing!

Mushers choose their smartest and speediest dogs to be at the front of the team. These "lead dogs" have a very close connection with their musher. Experienced lead dogs are often paired with those in training to show them how to act on the trail. Positive comments, such as "good dog," and treats reward new lead dogs for following commands.

It can take years to train a good lead dog—but it's worth it when mushers have strong dogs at the front of the team during a race!

ALASKAN HUSKY

Super Dogs

The best dogs for the Iditarod are a mixed breed called the Alaskan husky. These dogs are smart and easy to train. They're bred especially for speed and endurance. This dog breed isn't even recognized by the American Kennel Club as a true breed. Mushers don't care, though!

Mushers train with their teams all year. While summers are commonly too hot for Alaskan huskies to run in their harnesses, mushers take the dogs swimming or just let them run freely. By the fall, more structured training can start.

What about the mushers themselves? They have to be very fit and have a lot of mental focus. But training with the dogs, especially when winter comes and the dogs can pull sleds on the snow, is the best way for mushers to prepare for the Iditarod. They can practice using the brakes and communicating with their dogs, especially the leaders.

In Command

Mushers communicate with their dogs through spoken commands. Here are some of the most common terms heard on the trail.

mushing command	meaning
gee	turn right
haw	turn left
line out	pull the team straight out from the sled
whoa	stop
mush, hike, all right, let's go	start

Mushers run their dogs very long distances before the big race, perhaps as many as 3,000 miles (4,827 km). They may train with heavy vehicles other than sleds.

HAULING GEAR

There aren't many rules about sleds in the Iditarod. The rules state that each musher can choose any type of sled but that it "must be capable of hauling any injured or **fatigued** dogs under cover, plus equipment and food." Mushers are allowed to use up to three different sleds during the race.

The sleds aren't much different from those used in the past. They usually weigh about 100 pounds (45 kg), though that's doubled when carrying gear. They have big baskets for dogs to ride in and brakes. The musher stands on runners that extend out from under the basket.

Rope 'Em In!

All the dogs on a sled team have collars and harnesses connecting them to the ropes they use to pull the sled. The towline, or gang line, ties the dogs to the sled. The tug line ties the dogs' harnesses to the towline. The neck line ties

Sleds alone can cost hundreds or thousands of dollars.

Iditarod mushers must carry certain items, including a notebook used by the more than 35 **veterinarians** who take care of the dogs along the trail. Each musher packs a cold weather sleeping bag, an axe, and snowshoes, as well as eight pairs of booties to protect each dog's feet.

Veteran mushers carry much more than that. They bring extra pairs of boots, eye goggles, ski poles, and often a gun. They pack special wraps to ice dogs' sore limbs. Duct tape, a needle and thread, and tools like wrenches help mushers repair their sleds, harnesses, and lines, and even their own clothing.

Booties

Sled dogs have special footwear! Booties are meant to protect the dogs' feet from ice balls forming between their toes, sharp objects on the trail, and the heavy toll running can take on paws. Booties may be waterproof and have a bottom made of leather or other tough material.

One of the coolest things each team carries isn't gear—it's mail! Iditarod racers are given envelopes stamped in Anchorage and postmarked in Nome. These are sold after the race!

ON THE TRAIL

Each musher's experience during the Iditarod is different. Teams may purposely start out slow, or a musher may keep the dogs running at a consistent speed throughout the race. Some mushers run their teams at night and rest during the day.

While mushers can control their pace, one trail condition they can't control is the weather. Depending on the year, it may be too cold to travel safely—as cold as –60°F (–51°C). Or, it could be 50°F (10°C), making ice weak and the trail muddy and slushy. The race route is known for terrible snowstorms that can stop sled teams wherever they are!

Chowing Down

Sled dogs eat a lot! Mushers must be prepared with about 2,000 pounds (908 kg) of meat, dry dog food, and even fish and vitamins for their team during the Iditarod. More importantly, each musher carries a cooker and fuel to use it. The cooker melts snow to make water for the dogs to drink.

Iditarod racer Rudy Demoski prepares food for his team at a checkpoint in McGrath, Alaska.

CHECKPOINTS

According to the race rules, teams in the Iditarod have to take a full 24-hour stop at a place and time of their choosing. They must also take two 8-hour stops at certain points.

In addition, mushers take their dogs through checkpoints along the race route. These stops are very important for both the dogs' and musher's safety and health. Veterinarians look over the dogs and give any needed medical attention. If a dog is too sick to continue, it's left behind at these points to be cared for. Mushers and dogs eat and drink lots of water at checkpoints. Sled repairs occur at checkpoints, too.

A sled dog gets much-needed rest at a checkpoint.

The number of checkpoints and rests has increased over the years. There are usually 26 or 27 checkpoints, depending on the route taken.

Two Routes

During even years, the Iditarod uses a northern part of the Iditarod National Historic Trail. In odd years, mushers travel a southern section. This prevents the same small towns from having to deal with the impact of the race each year. It also lets the race pass through the old town of Iditarod every other year!

A DANGEROUS RACE

In 1984, Susan Butcher and her team fell through some thin ice! Though her lead dogs were able to pull them out, Butcher's experience shows how unpredictable—and dangerous—racing the Iditarod can be. For many, the riskiness itself is exciting. Still, a huge moose threatening a race team would probably cause even the most daring musher to be nervous.

Mushers pay a physical price during the race. Their hands become covered in **blisters**. Their wet, cold feet can freeze. If they don't sleep enough, they may start seeing things. One man let his body slam into a tree, breaking his collarbone, to avoid harming his sled!

Air Support

Iditarod daredevils aren't just on the trail—they're above it. The Iditarod Air Force helps supplies and **volunteers** get from place to place along the long race route. However, it's a dangerous job. The weather is often rough for flying. During the 2013 race, a pilot and his two passengers were killed in

Is the glory of crossing the finish line worth the physical hardships mushers face?

The dangers of the Iditarod affect sled dogs, too. Some become **dehydrated**, overheated, cut their paws, or get sick. For mushers, dogs' injuries or illnesses are part of the risk they take by competing in the race. But sometimes, dogs die.

In 2013, a 5-year-old dog named Dorado died after he was covered with snow overnight and couldn't breathe. His death was an accident, as sled dogs commonly sleep in snow to keep warm. However, Dorado isn't the first Iditarod death. In 2009, six dogs died. Two froze to death during a storm, while the cause of the others' deaths was uncertain.

When a dog is sick or injured, it's taken out of the race. About three dogs die in every Iditarod.

Animal Cruelty?

The Iditarod is tough, some say too tough on the dogs. People for the Ethical Treatment of Animals (PETA), a group that works for animal rights, calls the race the "I-hurt-a-dog." Though there's a rule stating that the dogs should be treated well, PETA reports that 140 Iditarod sled dogs died between 1973 and 2013.

TO THE FINISH LINE

About 400 people have finished the Iditarod, but some have done it in a spectacular way. In 1978, Dick Mackey and Rick Swenson raced into Nome right next to each other. Both no longer stood on their sleds' runners and were running next to their teams. When they crossed the finish line on Front Street, no one knew who won. An Iditarod official ruled that the nose of the lead dog from Mackey's team crossed the finish line first!

Dick Mackey's racing skills run in the family. His son Rick won the race in 1983. His other son, Lance Mackey, holds the current record for the most **consecutive** Iditarod wins at four!

Junior Iditarod

Thrill seekers come in all ages. In fact, mushers ages 14 to 17 can race in the 150-mile (241 km) Junior Iditarod! In 2005, Dallas Seavey became the first person to run the Junior Iditarod and the Iditarod in the same year. In February 2013, Noah Pereira, a 16-year-old from New York,

This team is running top speed to the finish line.
After 1,100 miles (1,770 km), victory is within reach!

In 2013, a dog named May got loose from her team. For 7 days, May's owner and local residents rode across Alaska in planes and snowmobiles looking for the dog. Sightings near the Iditarod trail were many, but they couldn't seem to catch up to her. Finally, a skinny dog with bloody paws was spotted quite far from the trail—it was May!

May's owner guessed the dog traveled more than 150 miles (241 km) before she was found. Based on where May had been sighted, she seemed to be trying to find the Iditarod starting line again. Clearly, mushers aren't the only ones who make headlines during the Iditarod! After everything you've just read about the Iditarod, can you imagine yourself as a thrill-seeking musher?

Yukon Quest

The 1,000-mile (1,600 km) race between Whitehorse in Yukon Territory, Canada, and Fairbanks, Alaska, might be even tougher than the Iditarod. The Yukon Quest follows a route once used by gold seekers and mail carriers. The race takes place in February, which means the weather is even more unpredictable than a month later during the Iditarod!

Another Iditarod veteran said May could have traveled 300 to 400 miles (483 to 644 km)!

GLOSSARY

blister: a painful swelling on the skin

consecutive: following one right after another

dehydrated: the state of not having enough water for the body to function well

emergency: an unexpected situation that needs quick action

epidemic: a large outbreak of a disease

fatigue: extreme tiredness

harness: straps around an animal that allow a driver to control it

musher: the driver of a dogsled

runner: one of the long pieces of wood, metal, or plastic on which a sled runs

technicality: a minor point that only comes to light after a very close look at rules

unpredictable: unable to be known in advance

veterinarian: called a "vet" for short, a doctor who is trained to treat animals

volunteer: a person who works without being paid

FOR MORE INFORMATION

BOOKS

Freedman, Lew. *Yukon Quest: The Story of the World's Toughest Sled Dog Race.* Kenmore, WA: Epicenter Press, 2010.

Hamilton, S. L. *Iditarod.* Minneapolis, MN: ABDO Publishing Company, 2013.

Hutmacher, Kimberly M. *Sled Dogs.* Mankato, MN: Capstone Press, 2011.

WEBSITES

Iditarod: Race Across Alaska
teacher.scholastic.com/activities/iditarod/index.htm
Find out more about the dogs, history, and trail of the "last great race on Earth."

Iditarod: Videos: Discovery Channel
dsc.discovery.com/tv-shows/other-shows/videos/other-shows-iditarod-videos.htm
Watch videos about training for the Iditarod and other cool topics on the Discovery Channel website.

Quiz Your Noodle! The Iditarod
kids.nationalgeographic.com/kids/games/puzzlesquizzes/quizyournoodle-iditarod/
How much do you know about the Iditarod? Test your knowledge on this website!

INDEX